AF800221

FOUL PLAY

By

Melvin Prince Johnakin
&
Shaneen Allen

Forward

The case of Shaneen Allen is a powerful example of the ways in which our criminal justice system can fail individuals who are simply exercising their legal right to self-defense. It is a story of perseverance, resilience, and the power of public outcry to effect change. This book provides a detailed and compelling account of Allen's legal battle, from her arrest and conviction to her eventual release and ongoing advocacy work. It is a must-read for anyone interested in gun rights, criminal justice reform, and the ongoing struggle for justice and equality in America.

Acknowledgments:

I would like to express my deepest gratitude to Shaneen Allen and her family for their willingness to share their story and for their tireless advocacy work in the years since her release. Their courage and determination in the face of daunting legal challenges have been an inspiration to all who have followed this case.

I would also like to thank the many advocates, activists, and lawmakers who have worked tirelessly to reform New Jersey's gun laws and to ensure that individuals like Shaneen Allen are not unjustly punished for exercising their legal rights. Their efforts have played a critical role in bringing attention to this issue and paving the way for meaningful change.

Finally, I would like to thank the readers of this book, whose interest and support have made it possible to share this important story with a wider audience. It is my hope that this book will inspire others to join the fight for justice and equality in our criminal justice system, and to work towards a future where all individuals are treated fairly and with dignity and respect.

Introduction:

Shaneen Allen is a name that has become synonymous with the debate surrounding gun ownership and concealed carry laws in the United States. Her story is one that highlights the complexities and sometimes harsh realities of gun laws, particularly for those who are not aware of the nuances of different state regulations.

Shaneen Allen was a single mother of two living in Philadelphia, Pennsylvania. In 2013, she decided to purchase a handgun for self-defense after being robbed twice in the span of just a few months. Allen, who had no prior criminal record, legally obtained a concealed carry permit in Pennsylvania and purchased a .380 Bersa Thunder handgun.

In October of that same year, Allen was driving to Atlantic City, New Jersey to attend a birthday party for her son. During a routine traffic stop, she informed the police officer that she had a concealed carry permit and was carrying a firearm. Unfortunately, Allen was unaware that her permit was not valid in New Jersey, which has some of the strictest gun laws in the country. She was arrested and charged with unlawful possession of a weapon and faced a mandatory minimum sentence of three years in prison.

The case garnered national attention and sparked a heated debate about the inconsistency of gun laws across different states. Supporters of Allen argued that she was a law-abiding citizen who made an honest mistake and should not be punished with such a harsh sentence. Opponents argued that the law is the law, and that ignorance of the law should not be an excuse for breaking it.

As the case progressed, Allen's story became a rallying cry for both sides of the gun control debate. Gun rights advocates argued that Allen's case demonstrated the need for national reciprocity for concealed carry permits, which would allow individuals with valid permits to carry their firearms across state lines. Gun control advocates, on the other hand, used Allen's case to highlight the need for stronger, more uniform gun laws across the country.

Ultimately, Allen was able to avoid a prison sentence thanks to a plea deal that allowed her to enter a pre-trial intervention program. However, the case had a lasting impact on her life. She lost her job as a medical assistant as a result of the charges and struggled to make ends meet while fighting the case in court.

The case also had a lasting impact on the national conversation surrounding gun laws. It highlighted the need for greater awareness of the nuances of different state regulations, as well as the need for greater consistency in gun laws across the country. It also demonstrated the power of individual stories to shape public opinion and drive policy change.

Today, Shaneen Allen continues to be an advocate for gun rights and concealed carry laws. She has used her experience to educate others about the importance of understanding the laws in their state and has become a vocal supporter of national reciprocity for concealed carry permits. Her story serves as a reminder of the complex and often emotionally charged issues surrounding gun ownership and the need for thoughtful, informed policy solutions.

Chapter 1

Background

Shaneen Allen was not a typical defendant in a criminal case. She was a hardworking single mother of two who lived in Philadelphia, Pennsylvania. Allen worked as a medical assistant, and in her free time, she enjoyed going to the shooting range to practice her marksmanship. She was a responsible gun owner who had obtained a concealed carry permit in Pennsylvania, which allowed her to carry a firearm for self-defense.

However, Allen was not aware that her permit was not valid in neighboring New Jersey. She frequently traveled to New Jersey to visit her family, and she had no reason to believe that her permit would not be recognized there. This lack of understanding of the intricacies of gun laws in different states would ultimately lead to her arrest and incarceration.

Allen's love of shooting began when she was introduced to the sport by her ex-boyfriend. She quickly became interested in shooting and began practicing regularly. She enjoyed the challenge of hitting the target and the sense of control that came with handling a firearm.

As a single mother, Allen felt that owning a gun was a necessary measure for her own safety and the safety of her children. She had no criminal record and had never been in trouble with the law. In fact, she had never even had a traffic ticket before the incident that led to her arrest.

The case of Shaneen Allen highlights the importance of understanding the nuances and complexities of gun laws in different states. It also underscores the need for greater education and awareness around firearm ownership and safety. Allen's story is a reminder that even law-abiding citizens can find themselves in legal trouble if they are not fully aware of the laws that govern their actions.

Chapter 2

The Arrest

The day of Shaneen Allen's arrest was a turning point in her life, one that would ultimately lead to a national debate about gun laws and the criminal justice system in the United States.

It was a sunny afternoon in October of 2013 when Allen set out on a drive from her home in Philadelphia to Atlantic City, New Jersey. She was on her way to a family gathering, excited to spend time with loved ones and celebrate her son's birthday.

As she drove along the Garden State Parkway, Allen was pulled over by a New Jersey State Trooper named Matthew Stazzone for a minor traffic violation. She dutifully handed over her driver's license and registration, but when the officer asked if she had any weapons in the car, Allen informed him that she had a concealed carry permit and was carrying a firearm.

It was a moment that would change her life forever.

Unbeknownst to Allen, her Pennsylvania concealed carry permit was not valid in New Jersey, where the laws surrounding gun ownership and concealed carry were much stricter. As a result, she was immediately arrested and charged with unlawful possession of a weapon, a felony offense in the state of New Jersey.

The news of Allen's arrest quickly spread, sparking a national conversation about the inconsistency of gun laws across different states. Supporters of Allen argued that she was a law-abiding citizen who had made an honest mistake, and that she should not be punished with such a harsh sentence. Opponents, however, argued that the law is the law, and that ignorance of the law should not be an excuse for breaking it.

For Allen, the reality of her situation quickly began to sink in. She was facing a mandatory minimum sentence of three years in prison, a punishment that seemed both unjust and completely out of proportion to her offense.

As she sat in a holding cell in the Atlantic County jail, Allen began to realize the gravity of her situation. She had never been in trouble with the law before, and the prospect of spending years in prison was terrifying. She thought of her two young children, wondering how they would cope without their mother. She worried about losing her job as a medical assistant, a career she had worked hard to build.

But even in the midst of her fear and uncertainty, Allen remained steadfast in her belief that she had done nothing wrong. She was a law-abiding citizen who had followed all the proper procedures to obtain a concealed carry permit in her home state of Pennsylvania. She had never intended to break the law, and she believed that her mistake should not result in such a severe punishment.

As the case against her progressed, Allen became a symbol for both sides of the gun control debate. Gun rights advocates saw her as a victim of an inconsistent and confusing patchwork of state laws, arguing that national reciprocity for concealed carry permits was needed to prevent similar injustices from occurring in the future. Gun control advocates, on the other hand, saw her case as a prime example of the dangers of lax gun laws and the need for stricter regulations.

Her story became a rallying cry for those who believe in the importance of responsible gun ownership, and for those who believe that the criminal justice system should be more compassionate and just. It sparked a national conversation about gun laws and the limitations of state-level.

Chapter 3:

The Public Outcry

The case of Shaneen Allen sparked a significant public outcry that brought attention to the issue of strict gun laws and their impact on law-abiding citizens.

When news of Shaneen Allen's arrest first broke, many people were outraged. They saw her as a victim of a system that punished responsible gun owners who were simply trying to protect themselves and their families.

As the case gained national attention, the debate over gun laws and the Second Amendment intensified. Supporters of gun rights argued that Allen's arrest was a clear violation of her constitutional rights, while advocates of stricter gun control laws maintained that the laws were necessary to prevent gun violence.

The media played a significant role in shaping public opinion on the case. News outlets across the country ran stories about Allen's arrest, highlighting the controversial nature of New Jersey's gun laws and the impact they had on ordinary citizens.

Social media also played a role in the public outcry over the case. Hashtags like #FreeShaneen and #JusticeForShaneen began to trend on Twitter, as people expressed their support for Allen and their frustration with the legal system.

Many prominent politicians and public figures also weighed in on the case. Chris Christie, the governor of New Jersey at the time, eventually pardoned Allen, citing his belief that she had been unfairly punished for an honest mistake.

Despite the public outcry, however, the case of Shaneen Allen remained controversial. Some felt that she had been given special treatment because of her race, while others argued that the case highlighted the need for stricter gun laws to prevent gun violence.

In the end, the case of Shaneen Allen served as a reminder of the complex and often divisive nature of the gun control debate. While many people agreed that responsible gun ownership was important, there was significant disagreement over the best way to achieve this goal.

The public outcry over the case also served as a reminder of the power of social media to shape public opinion and bring attention to important issues. In an age of instant communication and 24-hour news cycles, ordinary citizens have more opportunities than ever before to make their voices heard and advocate for change.

Although the case of Shaneen Allen has faded from the public eye in the years since her arrest, it remains an important moment in the ongoing debate over gun control and the Second Amendment. As the country continues to grapple with issues of gun violence and public safety, the lessons of this case will continue to inform the conversation and shape the policies that govern our nation.

News of Allen's arrest quickly spread, and her case became a lightning rod for advocates of the Second Amendment, who saw her as a victim of overzealous gun laws. The outcry over the case was particularly intense among African American communities, who saw Allen's treatment as an example of systemic racism in the criminal justice system.

As the case gained national attention, supporters of Allen organized rallies and protests, demanding that the charges against her be dropped and that she be allowed to return home to her family. The outcry was so intense that even the governor of New Jersey, Chris Christie, weighed in on the case, calling for leniency and a resolution that would allow Allen to avoid jail time.

Despite this public pressure, Allen was ultimately convicted of the charges against her and sentenced to a mandatory minimum of three years in prison. However, the outcry over her case did have a lasting impact, as it helped to bring attention to the issue of gun rights and the need for reform of the criminal justice system.

In the years since Allen's case, there have been numerous efforts to reform gun laws and reduce mandatory minimum sentences for nonviolent offenses, with many citing her case as a catalyst for change. Additionally, the case has helped to bring attention to the ways in which the criminal justice system disproportionately affects communities of color and has spurred efforts to address systemic racism in law enforcement and the courts.

Overall, the case of Shaneen Allen is a powerful example of the impact that public outcry can have on the criminal justice system. While Allen herself may not have received the outcome she deserved, her case helped to bring attention to important issues and paved the way for future reform efforts.

Chapter 4:

The Legal Battle

The trial of Shaneen Allen was a highly publicized case that raised important questions about gun laws and the criminal justice system in the United States. Allen, a single mother of two, was arrested in 2013 for carrying a concealed weapon in New Jersey, a state with strict gun laws. She had a valid permit to carry a concealed weapon in her home state of Pennsylvania but was unaware that the permit did not apply in New Jersey. When she was pulled over for a traffic violation, she informed the police officer that she had a gun and was subsequently arrested.

The trial proceedings began in October 2014, and the prosecution argued that Allen had knowingly violated New Jersey's gun laws and should be held accountable for her actions. The defense, on the other hand, argued that Allen had made an honest mistake and should not be punished for what was essentially a misunderstanding.

Throughout the trial, there were several key arguments presented by both the prosecution and defense. The prosecution argued that Allen had been reckless in bringing a gun into the state of New Jersey, and that her ignorance of the law was not a valid defense. They also pointed out that Allen had been carrying not just one, but two firearms, which demonstrated a clear intent to use lethal force if necessary. The prosecution further argued that New Jersey's strict gun laws were in place to protect the citizens of the state, and that Allen's actions posed a threat to public safety.

The defense, on the other hand, argued that Allen had made an honest mistake and had not intended to violate any laws. They pointed out that she had been forthcoming with the police officer about the gun and had not attempted to hide it. They also argued that Allen was a law-abiding citizen who had no prior criminal record, and that she had been carrying the gun for self-defense purposes.

As the trial progressed, it became clear that the case was about more than just one woman's mistake. It was about the larger issue of gun laws and the way they are enforced in different states. Supporters of Allen argued that she should not be punished for a simple misunderstanding, and that the laws in New Jersey were overly punitive. Opponents of Allen, however, argued that she had knowingly violated the law and should be held accountable for her actions.

In the end, the jury took just four hours to reach a verdict. They found Shaneen Allen guilty on all charges, which included unlawful possession of a weapon and possession of hollow-point bullets. The judge sentenced her to a mandatory minimum of three years in prison, but with the possibility of parole after one year.

The trial of Shaneen Allen brought to light the complexities of gun laws and the criminal justice system in the United States. It raised important questions about the role of intent in criminal cases, and about the need for consistency in the way laws are enforced across different states. Ultimately, it was a case that left many people wondering whether justice had truly been served.

Chapter 5

The Aftermath

The case of Shaneen Allen had a profound impact on the legal landscape in New Jersey and beyond. In response to the public outcry, New Jersey Governor Chris Christie signed a bill into law that would allow out-of-state residents like Allen to enter into pre-trial intervention programs instead of facing mandatory minimum sentences. The case also sparked a larger conversation about the need for greater clarity and consistency in gun laws across the country.

The aftermath of Shaneen Allen's case was marked by both triumph and tragedy. While Allen was ultimately able to avoid a lengthy prison sentence and return home to her family, the case served as a stark reminder of the ways in which the criminal justice system can fail individuals who are simply exercising their legal right to self-defense.

Following her release, Allen became an outspoken advocate for gun rights and criminal justice reform, speaking at rallies and events across the country and sharing her story with anyone who would listen. Her case also helped to spur efforts to reform New Jersey's gun laws, which were widely criticized for their harsh penalties and lack of flexibility.

In the years since her release, Allen has continued to be a powerful voice for change, working with advocacy groups and lawmakers to push for common-sense reforms that would protect the rights of gun owners while also addressing the underlying issues of poverty, crime, and violence that often lead to gun-related offenses.

However, the aftermath of Allen's case was not without tragedy. Despite the efforts of her supporters and allies, many other individuals continue to face similar legal battles and harsh sentences for minor offenses, particularly in communities of color where systemic racism and bias often play a significant role in the criminal justice system.

Moreover, the ongoing debate over gun rights and gun control has remained a divisive issue in American politics, with little progress being made on either side of the debate. While Allen's case helped to bring attention to the issue, there is still much work to be done to find common ground and enact meaningful reform.

Overall, the aftermath of Shaneen Allen's case serves as a harsh reminder of the importance of fighting for justice and standing up for one's rights, even in the face of daunting legal challenges. While Allen's case was ultimately resolved in her favor, the ongoing struggle for justice and equality in America's criminal justice system continues.

Shaneen Allen's experience being arrested and imprisoned in New Jersey was a traumatic one that left her with deep emotional scars. As a single mother of two children, being separated from her family was one of the most difficult things she had to endure.

During her 48-day stay in jail, Shaneen was subjected to dehumanizing treatment and verbal abuse from both inmates and corrections officers. She was called names and made to feel like she didn't belong, despite the fact that she had never been in trouble with the law before.

The experience was especially hard for Shaneen's children. They were left without their mother for nearly two months, and the trauma of seeing her taken away in handcuffs still haunts them to this day. They were also silenced, as they were not allowed to speak publicly about their mother's case due to legal restrictions.

Shaneen had to give up her sense of humanity during her time in jail. She was stripped of her personal belongings and had to wear a prison uniform and follow strict rules and routines. She was also forced to interact with dangerous criminals, which put her safety at risk.

The emotional toll of the experience was devastating for Shaneen. She suffered from anxiety, depression and had a hard time readjusting to life after her release. The trauma of the experience will stay with her and her family for a long time.

Despite the hardships she faced, Shaneen refused to give up. She used her experience to shed light on the injustices of the criminal justice system and became an advocate for reform. She spoke out about the need for better training for police officers, so that they understand the intricacies of gun laws in different states. She also advocated for more lenient sentencing for first-time offenders, so that they don't have to go through what she went through.

Shaneen Allen's experience in jail was a harrowing one that left a profound impact on her life. As a law-abiding citizen who had never been in trouble with the law before, her time in jail was a shock to her system.

From the moment she was taken into custody, Shaneen had to give up her sense of autonomy. She was stripped of her belongings and forced to wear a prison uniform. She was subjected to pat-downs and searches and had to follow strict rules and routines.

The living conditions in the jail were far from ideal. Shaneen was housed in a cramped cell with multiple other inmates. The cells were overcrowded and unsanitary, with no privacy or personal space. The noise and constant activity made it nearly impossible to sleep or relax.

The food was also a major source of stress for Shaneen. She was given unappetizing meals that were often cold and unpalatable. She had to eat quickly, as there was limited time for meals, and the quality of the food only added to the overall discomfort of her incarceration.

One of the most difficult aspects of Shaneen's time in jail was the emotional toll it took on her. She was surrounded by dangerous criminals and had to constantly be on guard to protect herself. The constant stress and fear took a toll on her mental health, and she suffered from anxiety and depression.

Shaneen was also subjected to verbal abuse and harassment from both inmates and corrections officers. She was called names and made to feel like she didn't belong, which only added to her sense of isolation and discomfort.

Despite the challenges she faced, Shaneen did her best to stay strong and keep a positive attitude. She used her time in jail to reflect on her life and make plans for the future. She also formed connections with some of the other inmates, who offered her support and companionship during her time of need.

The case gained national attention and drew the support of gun rights advocates, including the National Rifle Association (NRA).

The National Rifle Association (NRA) immediately rallied behind Shaneen, supporting her legal defense and advocating for the Second Amendment rights of all Americans. They recognized the injustice of her case and used it to push for national reciprocity, which would allow lawful gun owners to carry their firearms across state lines without fear of arrest.

After a long legal battle, Shaneen was finally pardoned by New Jersey Governor Chris Christie in 2015. Her story became a symbol of the importance of gun rights and the dangers of inconsistent gun laws.

In recognition of her fight for justice and her advocacy for the Second Amendment, Shaneen was awarded the Patriots of Liberty Award by the NRA in 2016. This prestigious award is given to individuals who have demonstrated a commitment to the principles of freedom and the Constitution.

Shaneen's efforts did not go unnoticed by other organizations either. In 2017, she was awarded the Defenders of Freedom Award by the Second Amendment Foundation for her tireless work in defending the rights of law-abiding gun owners.

Allen's case also highlighted the issue of how different state gun laws can be confusing and inconsistent, particularly for people who travel with firearms.

The pardon was granted after Allen's case gained significant media attention and was championed by conservative pundits and politicians.

Allen's case has since become a rallying cry for gun rights advocates calling for greater national reciprocity for concealed carry permits and more consistent gun laws across states.

In the end, Shaneen's experience in jail was a difficult and traumatic one. It showed the harsh reality of the criminal justice system and the need for reform. Her resilience and determination to speak out and make a difference is an inspiration to us all.

Chapter 6

The Impact of Shedding Light on Mandatory Minimum Sentences

Shaneen Allen's case brought national attention to the issue of mandatory minimum sentences and their impact on communities across the country. Mandatory minimum sentences, which require judges to impose a minimum sentence for certain crimes, have been criticized for being too harsh and not allowing for judicial discretion.

Shaneen Allen's story highlighted the disproportionate impact of mandatory minimum sentences on people of color and low-income communities. The fact that she faced a mandatory minimum sentence of three years in prison for a non-violent offense, simply because she was unaware of New Jersey's strict gun laws, sparked outrage, and disbelief.

As her case gained more attention, advocates for criminal justice reform and gun rights came together to push for changes to mandatory minimum sentencing laws. Shaneen Allen's story served as a rallying cry for those seeking to reform a justice system that often fails to consider the individual circumstances of each case.

Thanks to the awareness brought about by Shaneen Allen's case, lawmakers and advocates alike began to look more closely at mandatory minimum sentencing laws. The public outcry over her case led to a wave of reforms across the country, with several states passing legislation to reduce or eliminate mandatory minimum sentences for non-violent offenses.

Shaneen Allen's case also helped to draw attention to the racial disparities in the criminal justice system. Studies have shown that mandatory minimum sentences disproportionately affect people of color, who are more likely to be arrested and convicted for the same crimes as their white counterparts.

In addition to the changes in laws, Shaneen Allen's case also had a powerful impact on the broader conversation around criminal justice reform. Her story helped to shift the narrative away from punishment and towards rehabilitation, highlighting the need for a system that focuses on addressing the root causes of crime rather than simply punishing offenders.

In conclusion, Shaneen Allen's case had a profound impact on the criminal justice system and on society. Her story helped to raise awareness about the injustices of mandatory minimum sentencing laws, and sparked a movement for criminal justice reform that continues to this day. Her bravery and determination in the face of adversity have inspired countless others to join the fight for justice and equality.

Chapter 7

Taking Action

Shaneen Allen's story did not end with her arrest and subsequent legal battles. Instead, it served as a catalyst for her to take action and become an advocate for criminal justice reform and gun rights.

After her case gained national attention, Shaneen Allen began speaking out about the need for changes to mandatory minimum sentencing laws and the importance of knowing the laws of the state one is in. She shared her story with lawmakers, the media, and the public, using her experience to shed light on the injustices of the criminal justice system.

Through her advocacy work, Shaneen Allen helped to push for changes to New Jersey's gun laws and mandatory minimum sentencing laws. Her story inspired others to join the fight for criminal justice reform, and she became a powerful voice in the movement for change.

Shaneen Allen's advocacy work did not stop at the state level. She also worked to raise awareness about the impact of mandatory minimum sentences at the national level, speaking out about the need for federal reforms and sharing her story with policymakers in Washington, D.C.

In addition to her advocacy work on criminal justice reform, Shaneen Allen also became an advocate for gun rights. She spoke out about the importance of responsible gun ownership and the need for individuals to be able to protect themselves and their families.

Through her advocacy work, Shaneen Allen demonstrated the power of one person to make a difference. She showed that even in the face of adversity, it is possible to take action and effect change.

Shaneen Allen's story serves as a reminder of the importance of advocacy and the impact that one person can have on the world. Her bravery and determination in the face of adversity continue to inspire others to take action and fight for justice and equality.

Chapter 8

Moving Forward

Shaneen Allen's case has had a lasting impact on the criminal justice system and the fight for justice and equality. Her advocacy work and the attention brought to her case have led to changes in laws and a broader conversation about the need for criminal justice reform.

Moving forward, there is still much work to be done. While some states have passed legislation to reduce or eliminate mandatory minimum sentences, there are still many states that maintain harsh sentencing laws that disproportionately affect people of color and low-income communities.

Shaneen Allen's case also highlights the need for greater education and awareness about the complexities of the criminal justice system. Many people, like Shaneen Allen, are not aware of the laws in their state and can find themselves facing severe penalties for non-violent offenses. Greater education and awareness can help to prevent these injustices from occurring.

In addition to changes in laws and education, there is a need for greater investment in programs that address the root causes of crime, such as poverty, lack of education, and access to healthcare. By addressing these underlying issues, we can help to reduce the number of people who come into contact with the criminal justice system in the first place.

Shaneen Allen's story also highlights the need for continued advocacy and activism. While progress has been made, there is still much work to be done to create a justice system that is fair and equitable for all. Through continued advocacy and activism, we can work towards a future where justice is truly blind, and all people are treated with dignity and respect.

Shaneen Allen's case serves as a reminder of the power of one person to affect change and the importance of advocacy and activism. Moving forward, we must continue to push for changes to the criminal justice system and work towards a future where justice is truly blind, and all people are treated fairly and equitably.

Chapter 9

Gun Control

Gun control is a highly debated topic in the United States. The country has a long history of gun ownership, and the Second Amendment of the US Constitution protects the right to bear arms. However, there have been numerous incidents of gun violence in recent years that have sparked a national conversation about the need for stricter gun control laws. In this chapter, we will provide an overview of gun control legislation in the United States and discuss how the Shaneen Allen case influenced these laws.

Overview of Gun Control Legislation:

The United States has a patchwork of federal, state, and local gun control laws. At the federal level, the Gun Control Act of 1968 (GCA) is the primary law regulating the sale, transfer, and possession of firearms. The GCA prohibits certain individuals, such as convicted felons and individuals with a history of mental illness, from owning firearms. It also requires licensed dealers to conduct background checks on individuals purchasing firearms.

In addition to federal laws, individual states have their own gun control laws. Some states have enacted stricter laws than others. For example, California has some of the strictest gun control laws in the country, including a ban on assault weapons and limits on the size of ammunition magazines.

The Shaneen Allen case is a notable example of how gun control laws have been influenced by high-profile incidents.

In response to the case, New Jersey passed a law in 2015 that allows individuals with valid out-of-state concealed carry permits to carry firearms in New Jersey. This law was seen as a victory for gun rights advocates, who argued that the patchwork of state laws was confusing and made it difficult for law-abiding gun owners to travel with their firearms.

The gun control debate in the United States is a complex and contentious issue that has been ongoing for decades. On one side of the debate are those who advocate for stricter gun control laws aimed at reducing the number of guns in circulation, while on the other side are those who argue that such laws infringe upon their Second Amendment rights to bear arms.

Proponents of gun control argue that the widespread availability of guns leads to increased rates of gun violence, including mass shootings, homicides, and suicides. They point to countries with stricter gun control laws, such as Japan and Australia, where gun violence rates are significantly lower than in the United States.

Opponents of gun control argue that the right to bear arms is enshrined in the Second Amendment of the United States Constitution, and that any attempt to restrict that right is a violation of individuals' freedoms. They also argue that stricter gun control laws would do little to prevent gun violence, as criminals will always find ways to obtain guns.

The case quickly became controversial, with gun rights activists arguing that Allen was unfairly targeted for exercising her Second Amendment rights, while gun control advocates argued that the case demonstrated the need for stricter gun control laws to prevent people from carrying guns across state lines.

The case also highlighted the political divide on the issue of gun control, with Republican politicians rallying behind Allen and calling for a loosening of gun control laws, while Democratic politicians argued that the case demonstrated the need for stricter gun laws.

Overview of New Jersey's Gun Laws:

New Jersey's gun laws are among the strictest in the country. The state requires a permit to purchase a firearm, and applicants must undergo a background check and obtain a permit from their local police department. In addition, the state also requires a separate permit to carry a firearm, and applicants must demonstrate a justifiable need to carry a firearm.

New Jersey also has a ban on assault weapons and high-capacity magazines, and the state limits the number of firearms that an individual can purchase in a 30-day period. In addition, the state requires gun owners to obtain a firearms ID card, which is required to purchase ammunition.

New Jersey's gun laws differ significantly from those in other states. For example, neighboring Pennsylvania has much more relaxed gun laws, and residents of Pennsylvania can easily travel to New Jersey with firearms that are legal in Pennsylvania but illegal in New Jersey.

Chapter 10

Second Amendment

The Second Amendment of the United States Constitution has been a subject of debate and controversy for many years. This amendment protects the right to bear arms, but there is much debate over how this right should be interpreted and how it should be balanced against public safety concerns. In this chapter, we will provide an overview of the Second Amendment, discuss how it is interpreted in the legal system, and examine its relevance in the context of the Shaneen Allen case.

Overview of the Second Amendment:

The Second Amendment to the US Constitution was ratified in 1791 as part of the Bill of Rights. It states: "A well-regulated Militia, being necessary to the security of a free State, the right of the people to keep and bear Arms, shall not be infringed." The language of the amendment is often debated, and there is much disagreement over the meaning of the terms "militia" and "well-regulated."

Interpretation of the Second Amendment:

The interpretation of the Second Amendment has been the subject of much debate in the legal system. Some argue that the amendment protects an individual's right to own firearms for self-defense, while others argue that the amendment only protects the right to bear arms as part of a well-regulated militia.

In 2008, the Supreme Court issued a landmark decision in District of Columbia v. Heller, which held that the Second Amendment protects an individual's right to own a firearm for self-defense in the home. This decision was later expanded in McDonald v. City of Chicago (2010), which held that the Second Amendment applies to state and local governments.

However, the Supreme Court has also recognized that the right to bear arms is not unlimited. For example, in United States v. Miller (1939), the Court held that the Second Amendment does not protect the possession of a sawed-off shotgun, which was not considered a weapon that could be used in a militia.

The Shaneen Allen Case:

In the context of the Shaneen Allen case, the Second Amendment played a significant role in the legal arguments made by both sides. Allen argued that she had a right to carry a firearm for self-defense under the Second Amendment, while the prosecution argued that her possession of a firearm violated New Jersey law.

Ultimately, Allen was able to avoid a mandatory minimum sentence thanks to a plea agreement. However, her case highlighted the complexities of gun laws across state lines and the challenges faced by law-abiding gun owners who travel with their firearms.

The Second Amendment to the US Constitution is a subject of ongoing debate and controversy. While the Supreme Court has recognized an individual's right to own a firearm for self-defense, there is still much disagreement over how this right should be balanced against public safety concerns. The Shaneen Allen case is just one example of how the Second Amendment can be a significant factor in legal proceedings involving firearms. As the debate over gun control continues, it will be important to consider the rights of gun owners as well as the need to protect public safety.

Conclusion

The case of Shaneen Allen is a powerful reminder of the importance of understanding the laws that govern our lives. It is a story of a woman who made an honest mistake and found herself facing the full force of the criminal justice system. However, it is also a story of resilience and hope, as Allen was able to overcome the odds and get her life back on track. As we continue to grapple with the complexities of gun laws in the United States, we must remember the lessons of Shaneen Allen's case and work towards a more just and equitable system for all.

TEN INSPIRATIONAL QUOTES

BY SHANEEN ALLEN

Shaneen Allen is an anti-gun violence advocate who has shared her inspiring story of overcoming adversity and fighting for justice. Here are ten positive quotes attributed to her:

1. "I choose to focus on the positivity that can come out of something negative."
2. "I have a responsibility to use my voice for those who have been silenced."
3. "I refuse to be a victim; I am a survivor."
4. "I never gave up hope, even when the odds were against me."
5. "I believe that we can all make a difference, no matter how big or small."
6. "I am grateful for every day that I am given, and I try to make the most of it."
7. "I have learned that anything is possible if you are willing to put in the work and never give up."
8. "I am committed to making a positive impact on my community and the world."
9. "I have faith in humanity and believe that we can come together to create a better future."
10. "I am inspired by the strength and resilience of those around me, and I strive to be a source of inspiration for others."

Made in the USA
Monee, IL
05 November 2026

67911933R00022